Stay Healthy!

Why do we need to eat?

Angela Royston

www.raintreepublishers.co.uk
Visit our website to find out more information about **Raintree** books.

To order:
☎ Phone 44 (0) 1865 888112
▤ Send a fax to 44 (0) 1865 314091
▣ Visit the Raintree Bookshop at **www.raintreepublishers.co.uk** to browse our catalogue and order online.

First published in Great Britain by Raintree,
Halley Court, Jordan Hill, Oxford OX2 8EJ,
part of Harcourt Education.
Raintree is a registered trademark of Harcourt
Education Ltd.

Editorial: Jilly Attwood
Design: Jo Hinton-Malivoire, bigtop
Picture Research: Ruth Blair, Ginny Stroud-Lewis
Production: Severine Ribierre
Originated by Modern Age
Printed and bound in China by South China
Printing Company

10 digit ISBN 1 406 20046 8 (hardback)
13 digit ISBN 978 1 406 20046 1 (hardback)
10 09 08 07 06
10 9 8 7 6 5 4 3 2 1
10 digit ISBN 1 406 20051 4 (paperback)
13 digit ISBN 978 1 406 20051 5 (paperback)
11 10 09 08 07
10 9 8 7 6 5 4 3 2 1

British Library Cataloguing in Publication Data
Royston, Angela
Why do we need to eat?. - (Stay healthy!)
613.2
A full catalogue record for this book is available
from the British Library.

Acknowledgements
The publishers would like to thank the following
for permission to reproduce photographs:
Alamy p.7 top, 10, 12, 15(Loetscher Chlaus),
16(Jim West), 23a; Corbis pp.5, 19, 23e; Getty
Images pp7(bottom), 8(The Image Bank),
p.9(Photodisc), p.21 (Taxi); Harcourt Education
pp.4, 12, 23c (Gareth Boden), pp.6, 11, 13, 14,
17, 18, 20, 22, 23b-d(Tudor Photography).

Cover photograph of boys eating watermelons
reproduced with permission of Corbis. Back cover
images reproduced with permission of Harcourt
Education/Gareth Boden and Tudor Photography.

Every effort has been made to contact copyright
holders of any material reproduced in this book.
Any omissions will be rectified in subsequent
printings if notice is given to the publishers.

Our thanks to Dr Sarah Schenker, Dietitian, for
her help in the preparation of this book.

Some words are shown in bold, like this. You can find them in the picture glossary on page 23.

Contents

Why do you need to eat?

You need to eat because food gives you **energy** and **nutrients**.

Your body needs these to work properly.

You should eat lots of different kinds of food.

What do you need to eat the most of?

pasta

bread

potato

rice

Your body needs lots of food such as rice and pasta.

This is **starchy** food. Starchy food gives you **energy**.

Everything you do uses energy.

Who do you think is using the most energy here?

The children pushing scooters and riding bikes use the most **energy**.

The girl reading does not use as much energy.

You use energy even when
you sleep!

What food helps you grow?

Food that has **protein** in it helps you to grow.

beef

tuna fish

chicken

beans

All of these foods have protein in them.

Which of them is not meat or fish?

veggie burger

tofu

Beans are not meat but have **protein** in them.

Tofu and veggie burgers are made from a kind of bean.

cheese

Children need lots of protein because they are still growing.

Cheese has protein in it, too.

Why do you need food to keep you warm?

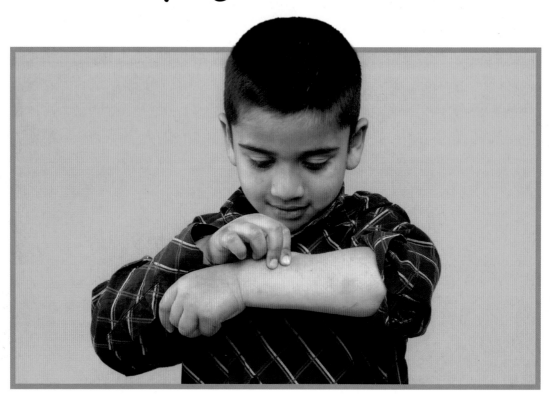

Your body stores extra **energy** from your food.

Some of this energy is stored as fat.

There is a layer of fat under your skin.

It helps to keep you warm.

Why do you need to eat fruit and vegetables?

Fruit and vegetables have lots of fibre.

Fibre helps your body to get rid of waste.

bread

broccoli

cereal

nuts

celery

orange

These foods have fibre.

Which of them are vegetables?

Celery and broccoli are vegetables.

Fruit and vegetables have **vitamins** and **minerals** in them.

Your body needs different vitamins and minerals to work properly.

What food makes your bones strong?

Food that has calcium makes your bones strong.

Does milk have calcium?

Milk, cheese, and yoghurt all have calcium.

Calcium makes your teeth strong, too.

Make some healthy coleslaw!

1. Wash some cabbage, a carrot and an apple.

2. Peel the carrot.

3. Grate the cabbage, carrot and apple.

4. Mix these in a bowl with some natural yoghurt.

5. Enjoy eating your healthy coleslaw!

Glossary

 **energy** what you need to move or do anything

 **mineral** kind of chemical that is in some foods that your body needs to be healthy

 **nutrient** chemical that is in food that your body needs to be healthy

 **protein** kind of food that helps you grow

 **starchy** type of food that gives you energy

 **vitamin** nutrient made by plants and animals

Index

Note to parents and teachers

Reading non-fiction texts for information is an important part of a child's literacy development. Readers can be encouraged to ask simple questions and then use the text to find the answers. Most chapters in this book begin with a question. Read the questions together. Look at the pictures. Talk about what the answer might be. Then read the text to find out if your predictions were correct. To develop readers' enquiry skills, encourage them to think of other questions they might ask about the topic. Discuss where you could find the answers. Assist children in using the contents page, picture glossary and index to practise research skills and new vocabulary.